Constructive Conflict
Building Something Good Out of All Those Arguments

By Keith R Wilson

Published by the Narrative Imperative Press

Printed in the United States of America
First Printing, 2015
ISBN: 978-1516822430

The Narrative Imperative Press
1596 Monroe Ave
Rochester, NY 14618
thenarrativeimperativepress@gmail.com

Table of Contents

Introduction

I've worked with all kinds of people in my psychotherapy practice, but, there's one thing they've all had in common: problems with conflict.

I've seen everyone from the worried well and the vaguely unhappy to the seriously mentally ill. Addiction, in all its variety, brings a lot of people in. People hooked on everything from water (yes, gallons and gallons of water every day), sex, gambling, and shopping, to heroin, crystal meth, and cocaine. Then there are the ones sent to me by girlfriends, parents, and probation officers for "anger management" as well as the girlfriends, parents, and probation officers, themselves. There are the depressed and anxious by the hundred and the traumatized by the thousand. About one-third of first appointments are couples, battling it out over one thing or another. I've had murderers, rapists, and child molesters in my office, as well as legions of their victims, separately.

CONSTRUCTIVE CONFLICT

You see, I've tried very hard, over almost thirty years or so, to avoid specializing in anything. I've wanted to deal with any problem that comes in the door. I want to be ready for whatever happens because people often, very often, don't know why they need to see a counselor. They think it's one thing, and they're right, it is, but it's also something else deeper or less readily identified or disclosed. I've added experts when I find that I am out of my depth, but I've never sent someone away with the message that I couldn't deal with them. Consequently, I've seen all kinds, and there's not a single kind that handles conflict well.

Interpersonal conflict, otherwise known as disagreement, dissension, argument, or strife, has been such a consistent issue for everyone that I have ended up specializing in it, despite my best efforts to not specialize in anything.

The problems people have in managing conflict fall into three types.

First, there are the obvious problems with conflict. The battling married couples who can't stop fighting; the anger management crowd, busting up everything from heads to china, the rapists, murderers, and child molesters, present conflict very plainly. No one disagrees that they have problems with conflict.

CONSTRUCTIVE CONFLICT

Less obvious are the people who dislike conflict so much they fail to speak up to confront injustices and exploitation. They permit themselves to be stuck in unsatisfying relationships, catering to the selfish and immature. They come into my office vaguely unhappy, so out of touch with their own feelings that they can barely think straight. They never come in and say they have trouble managing their anger, but they have anger management problems, also. They ignore their anger so much it turns it into anxiety, depression, and addiction.

The third group is the largest. These are the folks who bury their conflicts most of the time, like the second group, but find that things erupt, like the first, when they become mad as hell and can't take it anymore. They get locked into a vicious cycle, alternating between repression and reprisal. Their recurrent blow-ups give them justification to avoid the conflict that their lack of assertiveness generates.

The sad thing is, conflict does not have to be something to be feared. Conflict is the greatest hope we have. Unless you think everything is perfect, already: we need conflict so things can get better.

Mismanaged conflict is so universal that, at some point, I said there ought to be a book. I wanted to tell people, here, read this. We don't have enough time in the therapy hour to learn how to handle conflict constructively on top of everything else. It takes a considerable amount of repetition and practice to learn to do it well. Therefore, I would find a book, order boxes of it, and keep them stacked in my waiting room. No one would ever leave without one. There was just one problem with that plan, though: I couldn't find a book that would speak to the wide variety of clientele who come to my office. If there was going to be a book, I was going to have to write it.

Well, here it is. That's about all I want to say by way of introduction. You probably want to get right to it. You have conflicts, I know, and want to learn how to use them constructively.

CONSTRUCTIVE CONFLICT

Chapter 1
The Rock Tumbler:
Constructive Conflict in Action

I once knew a child who dug holes in his back yard. He would adopt stones that he liked and would line the shelves of his room with them. His mother used to complain of the grime he brought into the house, until, noting a sustained interest in geology; she got him a rock tumbler.

You may have had some dealings with a rock tumbler. It's basically a drum attached to a small motor by way of a belt that rotates incessantly all the live long day. Put a few dull, brown, craggy, soil caked rocks in the drum, add a bit of water, shut the hatch, turn on the motor, and you can keep the whole family from sleeping for a week. When your Dad yells at you to turn the damn thing off so he can get some rest, you open it, reach in, and your unremarkable stones have transformed into smooth, radiant gems.

10

CONSTRUCTIVE CONFLICT

There's a rock tumbler for people, too; a people tumbler. We call it love.

You think you're familiar with love, are you? It's the warm and cozy feeling you get when you look into your baby's eyes. It's the sweet sentiment you pick up in the greeting card aisle. It's the powerful talisman you utter on your third date that accelerates your circuit of the bases. Love sells wedding dresses, tuxes, gowns for the bridesmaids, bouquets, fancy cakes, and extravagant receptions. It also sells funerals, headstones, more bouquets, and extravagant coffins. It makes the world go around. It's a many-splendored thing.

As it often turns out, though, the warm and cozy feeling turns out to be little more than a glitzy advertisement on the package, a bait and switch scheme, a loss leader that lures you into the tumbler.

Love put you next to that snoring beast that snatches your covers in the night. It gave you to the shrew who wants you to put the toilet seat down for her, but won't put it up for you. Love made you the parent of that two-year-old having a temper tantrum in the grocery store. It showed you how to change your elderly parent's diaper. Love hitched you to the wife who hasn't gone down on you since your wedding night. It married you to the husband who won't talk about how he feels. Love is the thing that, when that maddening child, husband, wife, or parent dies, will make you keen over that extravagant coffin. Love is a many-splendored thing, isn't it?

Consider one maxim you learn every time you dicker at the market: Whoever has the most desire has the least power. If you want something bad enough and depend on someone else to get it, you have to meet them on their terms. Love is guaranteed to put you next to a person who does not share the exact degree of all your desires. In every pair, there is always one who is more horny, more messy, more spendthrift, more absent-minded, works harder, sleeps later, talks less, and is more likely to invite his or her relatives to stay for a week. That person will drive you nuts.

OK, so how does all that transform people into gems?

You could make like a cave man and bonk your woman over the head with a club every time you want sex, but she won't hang around and braise your mammoth. Instead, you learn some patience, some compassion, you write poems, go to movies that make you cry, play the guitar, watch the kids, and master foreplay. You wear your snoring bandage, learn to compromise, and it makes you a better man.

You could drag your husband to therapy and threaten divorce if he doesn't tell you about his feelings, but you won't like what he has to say. Instead, you discover that commitment is not something you declare on one bright, over-planned day, but something you perform every hour for a lifetime. You realize that trust and forgiveness are not nouns that describe states; they're verbs that indicate actions. You demonstrate tolerance, listen with your third ear, and cultivate understanding. You learn to agree to disagree.

You could push your elderly parent off on an ice floe and watch her drift away, but there'll be an ice floe ready for you someday. Instead, you listen to her stories and show her for the zillionth time how to make a call on an iPhone. You understand there is nothing new under the sun and wonders are not invented, so much as they are overlooked. You accept that even authority needs his diaper changed. You learn to hang on.

You could tie your children up and never let them leave the house, but you won't like what they say about you when you're gone. Instead, you teach them respect by showing respect for them. You realize that it's not possible to be a perfect parent, only, maybe, a good enough one. You acknowledge you have some growing to do, it is your child who will finish raising you, and he will do it by having a tantrum. You learn to let go.

Love can be operating in those relationships where you seldom admit it's present. You could pretend your roommate or the guy in the next cubical doesn't exist, but how will you ask him about that yogurt that turned up missing? Unless you're ready to steal his stuff, too, and enter into an escalating war of gotcha, you learn to speak up clearly, so that you protect your dignity, but respectfully, so he doesn't need to protect his. You wouldn't send him a valentine, but that's love, too. You can call it love whenever you soften when you could go hard or assert yourself when you're more inclined to sneak around.

Love could even be on the highway when someone cuts you off, in the comment section of a blog, or between lines of protesters who are shouting and waving placards. It could be, anyway, provided you treat the other like a human and permit yourself to be receptive, as well as challenging. You could go on, doing what you're doing and rail, ineffectively, at people you'll never change. Instead, you see their point of view so that you can solve problems together, rather than make new ones. It finally registers that we're all stressed, we all goof up, and we're all doing the best we can. You learn you don't need all that drama.

Love is the thing that'll push you to your limits. It'll take you outside your comfort zone, drop you off, and turn up the heat. Love is the means by which we evolved compassion, generosity, and empathy since those cave man days. It'll polish you up and make you shine.

That is, if you stay in the tumbler and rock.

That's what I call constructive conflict.

CONSTRUCTIVE CONFLICT

Chapter 2
Conflict

Here are a few major points that must be understood about conflict:

Conflict is inevitable. No two people are exactly the same or have precisely the same goals. No one will want to do the exact same thing at the exact same moment you want to do it, for the exact same reason every time. The fact that you have conflict does not mean your relationship is going down the tubes. Nor does it mean that you are incompetent in relating. It doesn't mean you're wrong. It doesn't mean he is wrong. Having conflict doesn't even mean you're having an actual conflict because a lot of times people are misunderstood. If you haven't had a conflict yet, you haven't been paying attention.

Communication increases conflict. Be careful of what you say if you come to my office for marriage counseling. If you say you want to communicate, I'll tell you to have a fight. No fisticuffs, or even F-bombs, are needed. Just start talking about the things you have never agreed on. Couples stop communicating when they want to avoid worrying their partner, upsetting him, or goading him. In other words, when they are avoiding conflict. If you want to communicate, and I hope you do, then you will have to talk about some of the hard stuff, the stuff that may cause a fight. If you don't want to communicate, then what are you doing here?

If you haven't had a conflict yet, you haven't really been talking.

Conflict is not the end of the world. Conflict is the beginning of a real relationship, not the end. Before you had your first fight, you were not seeing the real person. You were being too polite to be genuine. Your first fight brings you to a fork in the road. Take it.

Your choices are: You can leave the relationship and try to find someone you will not have a conflict with. You can silence yourself and tell yourself and tell her you don't want what you want. You can try to silence your partner. Or you can work this out.

If you work it out, then you learn that you **can** work it out. You can effectively compromise, acquiesce, and sacrifice something you love for someone you love. You know how to grow. That's a good thing to know, a good skill to have. The worse that could happen is that you might learn that you don't have to agree about everything.

If you haven't had a conflict yet, you haven't been real.

Conflict is like electricity: it can light things up, power change, or burn the house down. Conflict has so many positive attributes, that we just can't live well without it. We don't know what the issues are without it. Without conflict, if we automatically got everything we wanted, we wouldn't know the marinating flavor of deferred desire. If we could still just bonk each over the head every time we wanted sex, as in cave man times, we would have no need for poetry or music or flowers or fine food or any of the best fruits of civilization. If we could get our partner to fix the faucet as soon as we asked, we'd never learn to fix it ourselves. When you resolve a conflict through any means but force, you become a better person.

If you haven't had a conflict yet, you don't understand growth.

Violence is not conflict. Violence is conflict avoidance. The angriest person in the room is not the strongest, he's actually the weakest. People do not become violent when they feel capable and powerful. Capable, powerful people have no use for violence. People become violent when they're scared. They think they need a quick way out of the conflict, so they hit, or yell, or throw things, or punch a wall to get you to stop talking. If you're smart, you will stop talking, but it doesn't resolve the conflict.

You haven't had a conflict yet, if you've been violent.

CONSTRUCTIVE CONFLICT

Conflict can be regulated. In order to enjoy the benefits of conflict, you need to know how to have it without blowing everything up. You need to follow the regulations:

- Pay No Attention to the Alarm Going Off in Your Head
- Pick the right time and place.
- Start with the easy stuff.
- Stay relevant.
- Know what you're asking.
- Learn something.
- Acknowledge feelings.
- Call the four fouls of an unfair fight: defamation, defensiveness, stonewalling, and contempt.
- Don't be evil.
- Repair injuries.
- Detect dreams
- Compromise.
- Commemorate what you have accomplished.
- Practice

If you haven't had a conflict yet, you can't learn how to manage them.

Chapter 3

Pay No Attention to the Alarm Going Off in Your Head

The first thing you do when you come home, is turn off the burglar alarm, if you have a burglar alarm; so, the first thing you have to do to make construct use of conflict, is to disregard your alliance alarm. Yes, your alliance alarm. You have one. It goes off when there a perceived break in an alliance.

You see, you and your partner, as human beings, are social creatures. You're really not that good on your own and you know it, so you form alliances that enable you to accomplish things together that you couldn't accomplish alone. Each alliance is so crucial that you constantly monitor its health. You keep vigilance because you know that, if your ally turns against you, you're screwed. When you think you see something that indicates a break in the alliance, you get alarmed. The things you do then to try to correct it or protect yourself, create all kinds of trouble.

Basically, both you and your partner are constantly asking a single, basic, paramount, provocative question:

Are you there for me? And then you act fast on whatever you think the answer is.

It's a question that lies at the heart of every relationship. Why would you want to be in a relationship with someone who wasn't there for you? It's often the only reason you're in a relationship; to know that someone has your back: someone is at your side: someone has got you covered; you can stand on someone's promises; you are protected by someone.

This need is primitive and primal. It is baked in your bones. It's instinctual, seen in the youngest babies, who would not survive more than a day without someone taking care of them. It's a need you don't outgrow just because you put your big boy pants on.

Oh, you may think you're so independent and self reliant, but maybe the only reason you are is because you are secure in your attachments. You know that people are there for you, so you can afford to be independent.

It's so second nature that you monitor alliances without ever thinking about it. You do it constantly, with everyone, but particularly with the people you are the most connected to, with whom you have the most important unions. You know to the split second when there's a broken connection, but what you don't know is why there's a break, or how much of a break it is, or what part you played in creating it. You're not a mind reader, after all.

You also don't know how to talk about it. No one can explain what they do unconsciously or automatically. Try to explain the process of walking. You can't explain it as easily as you can do it.

It's also really hard to call someone out on a perceived alliance break without sounding hypercritical, or clingy, or paranoid. If you do, then you've created your own break. Therefore, if you're like a lot of people, you choose to withdraw emotionally, pretending that you don't need anyone. There's a break that your partner is bound to perceive, making the whole thing go around, and causing a shitstorm of perceived abandonment.

Chances are, every fight you've ever had with your partner was really a protest about emotional disconnection.

Your alliance alarm is going off when you complain that she doesn't put the toilet seat up. It's not the toilet seat, itself, that bothers you; it's the fact that she doesn't listen. Your alliance alarm is going off when he says, no, he doesn't want to have sex. It's not the lack of sex, itself, that alarms you, it's the fact that he won't engage. The alarm is going off when he works too much, when she won't tell you where she's been, when she pays more attention to her phone than you, and when you step into the TV room to tell him something important, he cranes his head to watch the football play. It's also going off in your partner's head when you complain of those violations. Don't you understand his commitments, trust her, want her to have other interests and admire his passions?

Your alliance alarm will go off when you try to address your conflicts. Disregard it. Notice I didn't say turn off the alarm. You can't turn off the alliance alarm; but, just as, when the smoke alarm goes off, if you are cooking, you won't run out of the house in your underwear, you'll turn down the stove.

Chapter 4

Pick the Right Time and Place for Conflict to be Constructive

If you read the last chapter about the benefits of conflict in a relationship, then you may be eager to have one. Hold your horses. Don't have one yet. Conflicts must be well regulated or there may be disaster. The first thing to consider is where and when to bring up the hard stuff.

If you remember all the difficult conversations you've had, some of them might have gone well, some not so well. We tend to blame things that go poorly on the people involved or on the issue. Maybe neither was at fault. Sometimes it's just the setting or the timing. Think back on the conversations that went poorly. Most often, you had attempted to conduct them at a time or in a place that was not conducive to success.

Consider, and talk with your loved one. Where would you and your partner rather have a conversation that might be difficult? There's no right answer. It's helpful to acknowledge what you and your partner prefer. Where would things go well?

- In a public place where you might be restrained, or a private place where you can talk freely?

- Looking at one another so that you can see reactions, or looking away, as in a car, where you are not so distracted by reactions?

- Sitting, so you can take your time, or standing, so that you might resolve things quickly?

- Touching, so you feel cared for, or not touching, so you don't feel clung to? How much touching? How about hugging? Hugging face-to-face or back-to-front?

- Should you be doing something with your hands, like cooking or eating, or put full attention to the conversation?

- Should there be potential weapons around? Do you need a referee?

In a similar way, consider and discuss the timing of when to have a difficult conversation so that it will go well:

- No one does well when they are tired, but when are you tired? Are you a morning person or an evening person? What's the optimal time of day?

- Most people don't do well when rushed, when there are other demands that need to be attended to, like children crying, phones ringing, dogs barking, a job waiting. Can you create a time to have a discussion that might resolve some differences?

- Vacations, get-aways, long car trips, even a weekend at home can be ideal to do this work with your partner. Have you had one lately? Do you need one?

- Or, would it be helpful to have a time limit on the discussion? Hard talks can be tough to take and some people can only tolerate them in limited doses. What's the optimal length for you and your partner?

- How do alcohol or drugs affect your ability to talk effectively? Can a little bit relax you and loosen your tongue? Or will it disinhibit you, so that you say and do hurtful things? Does it help you think and speak clearly?

- Do you do better if you know you will be having a discussion on a particular issue so that you can plan and think through what you want to say? Or, if you have the time to plan, do you just get worked up and stew?

CONSTRUCTIVE CONFLICT

Many times, when marriage counseling works, it has nothing to do with the skill of the counselor. It often works because the setting works for conversations. It's private enough so the whole world doesn't know your business, but you have a trained referee in attendance. You may sit or stand, look at each other, or not. Juggle a Koosh ball or hold a hand. Touch as much as you want as long as you are still talking. The time you spend in the counselor's office is bracketed, set aside for the issue. It ends at some point. You have to pay for the time, so you have an interest in making it worthwhile. However, you can't schedule a marriage counseling session every time you need to have a discussion. Sooner or later, you have to learn to do it yourselves.

As you consider these questions, there may very well be some factors that matter more to you than your partner. You might be a morning person; your partner doesn't come alive until noon. You might like to be touched; your partner may feel threatened if you touch her while you are discussing a disagreement. You might very well quarrel over where and when to talk about having a conflict. If that is the case, then you have an opportunity to compromise before you even start. Doing it her way may be a pretty good signal to show that you are interested in getting along.

The important thing is that you do not start a difficult conversation just anywhere or at any time. Do it in a thoughtful and considerate way so that all extraneous factors can contribute to success.

CONSTRUCTIVE CONFLICT

Chapter 5
Start with the Easy Stuff

I like to start chapters the same way people start conversations they know are going to be difficult. I like to get your attention at the very beginning by saying something outrageous or challenging. It's a good way to write, but, if you are starting hard conversations this way, you're doing it wrong.[1]

I'm sorry, I didn't mean to do make you feel bad.[2] I'm glad you're here.[3] I'm happy to be writing this book and actually have

---

[1] This is a good example of a hard start; something you should avoid doing when initiating a conversation with your partner. Discussions end on the same note they begin. If you start an argument harshly by attacking your partner, you will end up with at least as much tension as you began with, if not more.

[2] Now I'm going to try to show you how to start soft.

[3] Be polite

people who want to read it.[4] You may be enjoying it and learning a thing or two. I know I have, just from writing it.[5] Often I don't understand anything until I try to explain it to others.[6]

I think we can all agree that having a conflict with a person we love is fraught with difficulty.[7] I attempt to avoid conflicts when I can[8]. The result is that, when I can't avoid them, I may not know how to make a difficult conversation constructive.[9] I think we can also agree that some ways of starting those hard conversations work better than others. Coming in with guns blazing[10] gets me on the defensive. Does it do that for you, too? [11]

When you want[12] to have a conversation with me that might not go well and you begin by thanking me for my contribution, I can

---

[4] Express appreciation

[5] ... and gratitude

[6] Allow yourself to be vulnerable.

[7] Begin with something you all can easily agree on.

[8] This is an *I* statement. I am describing my own self. If I used the pronoun, *you*, you might object to that characterization and stop listening.

[9] Describe, don't judge.

[10] "Guns blazing" might be a value-loaded way of describing, but I like the image.

[11] Check to see if your partner is still with you.

[12] Here, I switch to "you" and try to describe clearly what I need

be more open-minded and we can resolve things without an argument.[13] When we begin by reviewing the things we already agree on, I feel I have something invested in a positive outcome.[14] I begin to see you as a colleague and not an opponent. When we work towards agreement on the easier stuff first, I am encouraged. It puts me in the right frame of mind to behave in a cooperative manner.[15]

Do you agree?[16]

---

[13] Observe the form: "If you... then I can... and we..."

[14] Be specific.

[15] Make one point at a time. Don't store things up and blast them with everything at once.

[16] Check in to see if your partner is still with you. Do it often and, especially, at the end.

CONSTRUCTIVE CONFLICT

Chapter 6
Now You Try Starting with the Easy Stuff

Think about a conflict you and a loved one have. Something that you've been meaning to talk about, but never find a good time. Something that you've talked about before, but always goes badly. If you're like most people, you will stew on it for days, weeks, months, or even years. Then, when you finally talk about it, it has fermented into a toxic, evil mess. It comes out of your mouth all wrong and you begin a fight even before you have begun talking. Now do it a different way. Practice here first.

1.Have you got an issue in mind? Good. Write it down. Express it the way you would naturally express it, before you started reading this book. Go ahead and throw up all that putrid bile you have inside you and put it on the page.

For example: *Every time my kids want something and ask me first, if I don't say yes, they'll go to their father, my god damn ex-husband, and ask if it's OK with him. Of course, he says yes, every time, and makes me look like a mean bitch and he looks like the fucking father of the year. He never wanted them in the first place and acted like a jealous two-year-old when they were babies.*

I think you would agree, if you started off a conversation with that, it would end up in a fight, but we're just getting started. Now you try.

2.   Imagine you're going to talk about it. Check your pulse. If it's racing, already, then take a few deep breaths and calm down. You haven't even started.

3.   Once you're calmed down, remember Chapter Three, when you determined a good time, place, and circumstance to talk about things. Where, when and how do you have your best conversations?

For example: *My goddamn ex-husband hates it when I bring things up when he picks up the kids, because he's in a rush to get going with them. All they do is go from one fun thing to another on their weekends, while I do the hard work of raising them. I guess, I'll have to make an appointment on his off weekends if I just want to have a fucking conversation. It's best if we do it in a public place, so we don't end up screaming at each other. At a coffee shop, so he doesn't start drinking, like he used to do.*

Now you try.

4.   Before you have this conversation, plan out how you're really going to start it. Remember the last chapter. Be polite, express

appreciation that your partner is there to work things out. Show some gratitude. Don't let it be canned. Make it real. The difference between canned gratitude and real gratitude is that you feel a little tingle when you express real gratitude. That feeling is you, being a little vulnerable. If you don't feel vulnerable, then you're not starting soft enough. Write a line, expressing appreciation.

For example: *Thank you for coming here to talk about the kids. It's important that we have these conversations from time to time, so we can be on the same page with parenting.*

Now you try.

5. Before you start talking about your disagreement, note the areas about the topic that you both agree on.

For example: *You never wanted the kids and acted like a jealous two year old when they were babies and I gave them more attention that you. Now they're at an age where they are fun and you have no problem spending time with them. We both agree that's important. We also agree it's important that they have everything they need, only you think they need more than I do.*

Guess what? I want you to try.

6. Now you should be ready for the real business, but your pulse should not be racing at this point. You just imagined a tender moment. If you're not feeling warm and fuzzy, then your partner

won't be, either. Don't go on with this exercise if you are not all warm and fuzzy. Go back and re-write so that you get softer and acknowledge more of the areas where you agree.

For example: *Before we start, I want to say that we both agree that the kids should be well taken care of. Neither of us want them to lack anything that's important. They should never have to wonder whether you'll be there for them. You've learned to be kind and generous to them.*

Now you try to soften it up, too.

7.Once you've talked about the areas you agree on, you're going to move on to the hard part of the conversation. Before you do, make sure your partner is still with you. Check in with him or her to see if they agree as much as you think they do. Ask him or her whether they are ready to move on.

For example: *This much we agree on. I want to talk to you about something I think is important. Are you ready?*

Write down in your own words.

8.Now go back to the initial statement that you wrote in #1, the one with all the putrid bile, festering on the page. You're going to edit it. First, address it to him. Next, look to see if you made more than one point. If you did, then cut out everything that doesn't serve that point. If you used any provocative or explosive words or images that would push your partner's buttons, get rid of them.

For example: *Every time ~~my~~ the kids want something and ask me first, if I don't say yes, they'll go to ~~their father, my god damn ex-husband~~ you, and ask if it's OK with ~~him~~ you. ~~Of course, he says~~ You say yes, every time, and make me look like a mean bitch. ~~He never wanted them in the first place and acted like a jealous two-year-old when they were babies.~~*

Now you take a crack at it.

    9.   Rewrite it so that you are describing his or her behavior, not his characteristics. Watch out for words like *always* and *never.* No one is always or never anything.

For example: *~~Every time~~ Sometimes the kids want something and ask me first. If I don't say yes, they'll go to ~~their father, my god damn ex-husband,~~ you and ask if it's OK with ~~him~~ you. ~~Of course, he says~~ When you say yes, ~~every time, and~~ it makes me look like a mean bitch.*

    10. Look to see if you are being vague anywhere. Change it so that you are being specific.

For example: *~~Sometimes~~ Last Tuesday, ~~the kids~~ Brittany and Sam ~~want~~ wanted ~~something~~ me to take them to the water park. ~~and ask me first, if I don't say yes,~~ I told them they couldn't go because they didn't clean their rooms. ~~they'll go to you and ask if it's OK with him~~ I understand they asked you last Saturday. When you took them, it*

~~makes~~ *made me look like a mean bitch.*

Try it.

11. If you're complaining about something he or she does, then summarize it in the form of an *I Statement. I Statements* go like this:

I feel _____ when you _____, if you
_____, then I can _____, and we
_____.

For example: *I'm feel scared the kids are going to think I'm just being mean when I give them consequences. If you could check with me first, I can tell you the reasons I said no and we can do a better job of raising them to be responsible.*

Now you try.

You should now have a script of how to start a difficult conversation so that it will prove to be productive. It'll get easier and more natural with practice. This is just the beginning. There are still a lot of things that can go wrong from this point, but, at least, you have started things off on the right foot.

Chapter 7
Be Relevant

If you have a conflict with your partner, be sure it has something to do with your partner.

Let me illustrate.

Sam's wife asks him to take out the garbage. It's a reasonable request. Someone has to do it and it might as well be Sam. But he snaps at her. An argument ensues. It's not the garbage that he minds so much, it's the asking. There's something about being asked that bothers him.

Sam's mother used to ask Sam to take out the garbage, too, but she didn't ask nicely. She would beat him if he didn't do it right away. He's angry about that still, even though he hasn't thought about it in years.

He managed to survive childhood and grow up and get married. It was all good until his wife asked him to take out the garbage. Something about it subconsciously reminded Sam of his mother. He didn't realize he was responding to his wife in the way that his mother deserved, but that's what he did.

When his wife innocently asked him to take out the garbage, Sam's mind automatically went to his memory bank for something like this experience before. He pulled an old file. There were emotions stored there that escaped when he opened it.

Any time our emotions are out of proportion to the issue at hand, as Sam's were when his wife inoffensively asked him to take out the garbage, the 20/80% rule is at work. Twenty percent of what you are upset about has to do with the here and now situation. Eighty percent has to do with what's in the files. In this case, twenty percent of the need to snap came from Sam being annoyed at having to take out the garbage. Taking out the garbage is annoying. It's tiresome, it smells, and he has to put on his slippers, but twenty percent of a snap is hardly anything at all. It might be a sigh or a groan. That's it. In this case, the other eighty percent of the snappage came from unresolved anger at the way Sam's mother treated him. He has good reason to be angry, but not at his wife. She didn't beat Sam.

Sometimes it's a simple matter of sitting down and consciously looking at what's in the files. I do it all the time with people who come in for therapy. Often it's just a matter of asking, *when have you felt that way before?* and everything in the files comes out. It doesn't have to be extreme abuse. I then explain the 20/80% rule. People get it. It would be easy for Sam to see that he's letting his wife have it for something his mother did. Most of the time it's enough to be aware that you're doing it and eighty percent of the upset about the present situation goes away, just like that.

Sometimes it's harder to see what's in the files. There are some cases where the people just don't want to look, it's too painful. Unfortunately, the files affect them whether they want to look or not.

In other cases, the material in the files was placed there before the child had the ability to use language. Then, what is placed there cannot be accessed by words. They are raw feelings, what we call body memories.

In these tough cases it's often enough just to know that there are horrible things in the files. We may not need to know the details of the horrible things to let them go.

Whenever you're reacting out of proportion to what your partner has done, you can bet that eighty percent of your reaction has to do with something in the past that is in your files. It is possible to let go of that horrible material, whatever it is.

That leaves the remaining twenty percent. This is the proportion of the problem that your partner can do something about. That's the part you bring to the table in conflict. The rest is beyond anything you can do with your partner. It should either be let go or addressed with the person responsible for the trauma in the files. Let go of the portion of things your partner can do nothing about.

Chapter 8
Know What You're Asking

Sometimes you have questions. If you do, work out what those questions really are, or the answers you get may fail to satisfy.

You might start asking the wrong questions if you suddenly find out about something your partner has been doing for some time, like an affair, an addiction, or, when you thought he'd been going to work each morning when he really has been going to the unemployment office. To look at a single example, let's say you just found out your wife's been having an affair with some guy. You start asking questions.

Who was it? Where did you meet him? When did you see each other? What did you say to one another? How many times did you have sex? What did you do when you had sex? How was it? Did you orgasm? And so on and so forth.

If she fails to answer those questions thoroughly, you get the feeling she's holding something back, being evasive, stuck in denial. However, if she gives you the answers then you have some vivid and explicit images that you can't get out of your head. Many, many partners have rued the day they asked those questions.

What is it that you really want to know when you ask those questions? Do you really want to know if he made her come and how he did it? Is it important that you document that the text she got while you were celebrating your anniversary, was sent by him and was filled with xxx's and ooo's? What will you do if you know his identity? Will you find him and punch him out, or will it reassure you it wasn't some other guy? If she does give answers, then how do you know that she's being truthful? How can you believe her, anyway?

You see where I'm going with this? They may not be the right questions. Try to reformulate them. What is it that you really want to know?

Let's try this one, a question that I believe lies under all the others.

Can I trust you?

Now we're getting somewhere. This may be closer to the heart of the matter. You're asking all these questions that require unequivocal answers because you are putting her to the test. You want to see how revealing she can be. It's not that you actually want the information, you want to see candid behavior. You want it out on the table, no holds barred, complete honesty and straightforwardness. The more explicit the answers, the more you will be able to trust her.

She can only do so much, though. *Can I trust you?* is not a question she can answer completely. It's a question you need to ask yourself. She could tell you everything. Every single sordid detail, and you would still wonder, *Did she tell me everything?*

The feelings you're having, like any feelings, are yours. It's up to you whether you feel them or not. I'm referring to that feeling like you've just been punched in the stomach. The feeling that you're out of breath. The feeling that you're dizzy and about to pass out. They may have appeared after you learned she had been cheating on you, but these are your feelings. Take a few deep breaths, do something distracting, think of something pleasant, and they'll go away for a minute. When they return, do it again.

When you're asking, *Can I trust you?,* you're really asking, *What will I do now?*

Well, that's up to you.

Here's another question that might have been imbedded in all the questions you had.

You hurt me, can I hurt you back?

That train you felt hit you when you heard she was having an affair, you want her to feel it, too. So, you extract a confession, force her to recount, in detail, the most shameful moments of her life, confront her with times and dates and actions, just to make her squirm like she made you squirm. You won the moral high ground, so you plant your flag and beat your chest and never let her forget it. You have power over her, so you collect it, hoard it, and demonstrate it through torture and inquisition. If she puts up with this, then you know she really still loves you.

The answer to the question, *Can I hurt you back?* is, of course, yes. The more you love someone, and the more they love you, the more you can hurt each other. However, if you love someone, why would you want to?

How about this one?

What's wrong with me?

You believe that she would not have had that affair if she had been satisfied at home. You think that, if you were enough of a man to keep her, you would not have lost her. You wonder if the two of you have had some problems that she never talked about, if you were ever meant to be together. You know that you could do better, you could change, if only you knew what to do.

This question can give you valuable information that you can use to work on yourself and your marriage or it can put you on the road to complete masochism. It can take the focus off her and what she's done and put it on you. Some of the focus needs to be on you, affairs don't happen in a vacuum, but maybe the issue has been your narcissistic need to always be the center of attention. Not everything is always about you, you know.

What's wrong with me? is a question that's closely related to the next one.

Why?

Why? is a good question, but it's not one that she will likely be able to answer, especially in the beginning. You may need help with this question from someone like me.

Then there's this question:

Will you let me in?

People in close relationships need to have a reasonably accurate map of the inside of each other's head so they can understand their partner's perspective and predict their desires and behavior. If you're just learning now that she had an affair, or, for that matter, an addiction or a secret unemployment, then it is apparent that you have not downloaded an updated version of this map.

To have a good map of the inside of your partner's head, you have to spend some time in there. You need to meet the people she spends time with, understand her daily routines, know how she feels about things, see what her worries are, apprehend her dreams, and what turns her on. If you played *The Newlywed Game,* you should be able to win.

To have a good map, you need to talk. You need to talk about more than just the affair.

One more revision of the questions.

Can we get on the right track?

That is a good question, but it's another one that cannot be answered by talking. It has to be answered by doing. The way to get on the right track is to ask the right questions and for her to give candid answers. Give some consideration to your questions. Ask honest questions to get honest answers.

Chapter 9
Learn Something

You keep having the same argument with your partner. You're always going around in a circle, on and on and on. You never get anywhere, never resolve anything. You're getting sick of it, and maybe a little bit sick of her. What are you doing wrong?

You're not learning anything.

Remember what school was like? You sat at a desk and listened to the teacher. You squirmed in your seat until recess came. You formed groups and made presentations. You wrote papers, completed equations, started art projects, and sang songs. You groaned about all the homework you had and came up with creative reasons you didn't complete it. You went up to the board. You raised your hand. Remember all that?

If that's all you did in school, you didn't learn a thing.

School also involved taking tests, receiving grades, getting told by the teacher if you were right or wrong. You had to have feedback to know whether you were on the right path. Without it, you'd get lost.

If you didn't have feedback, you wouldn't learn. If you thought you learned, you couldn't be sure you got it right.

If all you are doing when you have an argument with your partner is telling her how you feel, then you are not learning anything. If all you are doing is answering her questions or responding to her accusations, then you are as clueless at the end of those conversations as you were in the beginning.

If you do not have feedback from your partner, you're not learning a thing.

You should never have a serious conversation without inviting feedback. Never say anything to your partner, without having her demonstrate that she understands it. Never assume you know something she's trying to say without checking with her first.

You've seen it in the movies.

The captain, anxious to avoid the iceberg, shouts to the helmsman, Hard right rudder!

The helmsman, before he does a thing, answers back, Hard right rudder, Sir.

That's feedback. Checking that you understand something before you proceed.

Let me show you how it works in a marital context.

Your wife comes home from work and says to you, "I work all day while you're home playing video games. The least you could do is pick up the house and make dinner so I don't have to do it."

Your wife, in this example, has not yet learn the soft start.

You might have a lot to say about that. You may have a retort ready. You don't play video games all day. Your two year old just made that mess in the past ten minutes. You were going to take her out for dinner. You might want to attack, call her a bitch, bring up something she does that annoys you. All those things would start a fight, or continue one.

Before you do any of those things, check to see if you heard her right, first.

Say something like this: "You want me to pick up the house and make dinner for when you come home because you think all I do is play video games. Is that right?"

You are not agreeing with her or conceding. You are not accusing her of something or starting a fight. You are simply reflecting back what you thought she said.

She may say, "Yes, that's what I'm saying. It's about time you listened."

She might make some minor correction because you didn't hear it right or she didn't say it right. Most of the time, giving feedback de-escalates the situation. She's likely to back down from her original statement.

"No, honey, I realize you do more than play video games all day. I'm just tired, I guess."

Doesn't that sound better than a fight?

Chapter 10
The Talking Stick

There's an object in my office I want to tell you about. It's a Talking Stick.

No, the stick doesn't talk. You do when you hold it.

The concept of the Talking Stick comes, I've been told, from an old Native American tradition. When the elders gathered in a teepee to talk about important matters, they would pass a Talking Stick around. Whoever had the stick had the right to speak. Everyone else listened.

There are characteristics about sticks that make them perfect for talking. A stick performs the same functions that words can. A stick can be used for support. It can point things out. It can be a weapon. Your words are the same way. Your words can also support, point things out, or be used as a weapon. When you are handed a Talking Stick, you are being trusted that you will use your words wisely.

CONSTRUCTIVE CONFLICT

My Talking Stick has some feathers on it. When you hold the stick and speak, the feathers will move, blown around by the wind your breath makes. This is to show that your words have effect. People can be stirred, affected, or blown over by your words.

I attached a small bag of stones to my Talking Stick. Stones that have been through my rock tumbler. I told you about the rock tumbler in chapter one. The rock tumbler is my favorite metaphor for relationships.

The Talking Stick is best held so that the bottom end is resting on the ground. That's to symbolize that the talker is grounded. He or she is connected to reality, that Earth upon which we all stand. However, the point only touches a very small piece of the Earth. The talker can only claim a small bit of reality, just the point he or she is trying to make at the moment.

I frequently use the Talking Stick in marriage counseling whenever the partners have something they need to learn from one another. You may remember in the last chapter I said that if you are not getting feedback, you are not learning anything. When you use the Talking Stick properly, you get feedback; you can learn.

Whoever starts off with the stick gets to speak first, but, but just as the stick can only point to once place at a time, you can only make one point at a time. You can't go on and on and on and expect that your partner can absorb it all, must less show comprehension, and respond to everything at once. Keep it short and concise.

Once you've made your point, your partner has to earn the right to speak by demonstrating that he has understood what you have just said.

Your partner should paraphrase the point you just made, not parrot. It's possible to mindlessly repeat what you've just said without understanding it. Paraphrasing is harder. Paraphrasing requires that he put into his own words the gist of what you were trying to say. He should paraphrase everything you just said when you had the stick.

If you asked him a direct question, he should paraphrase the question before answering it. That's so he can prove to you and to himself that he understands the question he's answering. Otherwise, he could be answering a question you didn't even have. What good is that?

When you are satisfied that your partner comprehends the point you made, then you give him the stick. Even if he doesn't agree, you can be satisfied that he gets it. He knows where you are coming from.

If you're not satisfied that he understands, you have to make your point again, in a different way. Maybe he wasn't listening. Maybe he distorted what you were trying to say. Maybe you weren't explaining things well. Maybe you two have a variance over the meanings of words. In any case, aren't you glad you asked him to paraphrase? If you hadn't, then you might have gone on in a confused manner.

When he gets the stick, be prepared; you will have to paraphrase when he is done.

My Talking Stick has a lot of spiritual medicine from hundreds of people talking with it over a quarter of a century. You'll have to make an appointment if you want to use it. If you can't make an appointment, it's easy enough to make your own. However, you would have to provide your own spiritual medicine.

Chapter 11
Acknowledge Feelings

Every communication has two parts. There's the words and there's the music. There's the content of what you say, and there's how you say it. There's the thought expressed, and there's the feeling.

In the last two chapters, I've been writing about how giving and receiving feedback is an essential part of working through conflict. It's necessary to demonstrate that you understand what your partner is trying to say before you can be sure you understand it. You need your partner to demonstrate understanding before you know that she gets it. You might think that if you just paraphrased her words correctly you have grasped the message. Often that's not the case. Many times it's the emotion that she is most interested in conveying.

So, your wife comes home from work and says to you, "I'm sick of it! I work all day while you're home playing video games! The least you could do is pick up your shit so I don't have to do it! And where's dinner?"

If you were to paraphrase just the words, you might say something like this, "You want me to pick up the house and make dinner for when you come home because you think all I do is play video games."

That paraphrase is likely to be technically correct, but misses the main point. It fails to grasp the sense of urgency she's trying to express. If you were to paraphrase the emotions as well as the words, you might say, "You're angry and disgusted with me because you think all I do is play video games. You'd like me to pick up the house and make dinner, instead."

See, you reflected back what you thought you saw in her emotions, that she was angry and disgusted. You didn't agree with her. You didn't say, Yeah, I know, I'm a lazy and disgusting pig. You simply acknowledged her emotions. This is important for a number of reasons.

First, you are reacting to her emotions as well as her words. When she comes in the door and screams, you would react differently than when she says those same words sweetly, right? Therefore, you would want to check out your perception of her emotion to see whether it is correct.

Secondly, she's trying to say something with her emotions as well as with her words. When you acknowledge the emotions, when the message is accurately received, she may have no reason to continue to express them. Most of the time when emotions are acknowledged, people can let go of them. She won't need to convince you that she's angry anymore, when you show that you understand her emotions.

Finally, people's thoughts and emotions are often out of sync. When you acknowledge her emotions, it's like you are putting a mirror up to her and showing her just how she looks to you. She may not realize she's coming across so strong. This might help her tone it down a bit if she doesn't mean to come across as a raving maniac.

If she wanted to come across as a raving maniac, then you have let her know that you got the message.

So, acknowledge the emotions as well as the thoughts, even if, especially if, you don't agree with them.

CONSTRUCTIVE CONFLICT

Chapter 12
Calling Fouls

Any marriage counselor can sit with a couple and listen to them talk about a difficult issue for three minutes and know whether they are heading for a break up. All the counselor has to do is spot fouls. The fouls predict that a conversation will not be productive. It may turn into a fight. An accumulation of fouls often results in divorce.

The four fouls most prophetic of trouble are defamation, defensiveness, stonewalling, and contempt. We will look at each of them in detail in later chapters, but for now, let's talk about how to call them.

What should you do if you spot a foul? All it takes is one and a conversation will begin to deteriorate. Nothing good will come of talking any more unless the foul is addressed.

It's best when you can call the foul you're guilty of committing. If you're talking with your partner and you catch yourself defaming her, getting defensive, retreating into silence, or expressing contempt, you should stop right there and admit your mistake. It's time to re-boot.

I admit it's sometimes hard to notice when you are fouling. Many people were raised to foul. The relationships they saw when they were growing up were dangerous places where family members committed flagrant violations so frequently they were routine. If that was the case, you know you don't want to continue the tradition. You probably swore to yourself you would never do as your parents had done. Well, now's your chance. Pay attention when it happens, when you open your mouth and the words of your violent father or shrewish mother come out. When you catch yourself, or your partner catches you fouling, stop, apologize, and start the conversation over.

If you know you're committing a violation and you do it anyway, you are behaving as if you're a sadistic prick, unworthy of human companionship. I know those are harsh words, especially coming from a therapist type, but I've witnessed enough pain in my office that I want to call out the conduct that inflicts it. However, I am enough of a therapist to know that just because you behave like a sadistic prick, doesn't mean you are one. As a matter of fact, I don't think I ever have met a real sadistic prick, only people who sometimes act that way. All the more reason to take responsibility for the violations you commit, seeing as though they are so out of character.

So, what do you do if you spot your partner committing a foul that he doesn't call on himself? He might've been aware of it and needs you to point it out. It's vitally important that you don't just let it pass and ignore it as if it never happened. The conversation may deteriorate into a fight if you go on that way and you will certainly not get your issue resolved. If he is not aware of the violation, he will not learn that he is fouling and will go on to do it again. It's possible to create a monster out of a perfectly good human being by letting him behave in a selfish, childish manner.

Therefore, it's important to call fouls that your partner does not call on himself. Do it like this:

- *Try again.*
- *I am getting scared.*
- *Please say that more gently.*
- *That felt like an insult.*
- *Let's start over.*
- *Let's take a ten minute break.*
- *Let's calm down.*
- Use an already established safe word.

Or, if you can do it in a humorous way:

- *Foul*!

- Throw a yellow handkerchief

- Blow a whistle

- I know a very modest couple; every time one of them spots a foul, he or she takes off a single article of clothing, starting with a watch, or a belt, or a single shoe, whether they are in public or not. It doesn't take long before the conversation straightens out.

•

Chapter 13
The First Foul:
Defamation

Defamation is the first foul to look out for when you are attempting to have a constructive conversation. It often comes in the opening salvo, right when a serious discussion is initiated. It gets the partners off to a terrible start, and things just go downhill from there.

Defamation is a false statement that disfigures the character of your partner. It occurs when you take normal complaints and turn them into pronouncements about your partner's personality.

You might recognize defamation from back in **Chapters Four and Five** when we looked at how to initiate a conversation, although I didn't use the term there. It's such an important concept that I thought we'd look at it again.

You might have this normal (but, trivial) complaint: "I like it when the toilet paper is put it so that it feeds from the top of the roll, not the bottom. It tears more easily when it feeds from the bottom and all I get are these small pieces. Would you please put it so it feeds from the top?"

If you utilize defamation, the complaint goes like this: "You're always putting the toilet paper so it feeds from the top. You never listen to me. You know I don't like it that way, but you do it regardless. You're selfish and inconsiderate."

Defamation imputes something horrendous about your partner's character and distorts reality for dramatic effect. It comments on your partner's nature, rather than his deeds. It turns what could be a simple request about a minor annoyance into major drama.

Listen for a few key words and tricks to spot defamation.

You're always... You never...

No one always or never does anything. Never. There are always exceptions to every rule. (Even the rule that there are exceptions to every rule, I suppose.) You're not following your partner around constantly, how do you know how he installs the toilet paper roll when he's at work or at someone else's house? Maybe he used to do it your way when he was a kid, until he found a method he thought worked better? Since you don't know, you may be saying it that way because you're trying to pick a fight.

You never listen ... you know...

Just because he doesn't change his behavior when you ask him to doesn't mean he isn't listening. He may not have heard you or understood you. When you taught him the correct way of installing toilet paper, did you ask for feedback so that you could check that he learned what you tried to teach him? How do you know whether he knows or not? He may have his own reasons for doing it his way and never got a chance to explain it to you. Furthermore, his listening and knowing are subjective experiences, out of reach of your capabilities.

You are...

Defamation often uses the verb *to be* in many of its declinations: *You are, he is, we are, they are, you were, he was, they were.* The state of being is not a static condition. Whenever we use this verb, we distort reality to a degree. People are just not as constant as the verb suggests. Your partner knows this about himself. He has far more experience with himself than you have with him, so don't kid yourself into thinking you know what he does about toilet paper rolls better than he does. This is one argument you cannot win.

If you use defamation, you'll get into an argument, or worse. He just might decide it's not worth talking to you. If the discussion is going to be about his character, he might commit some fouls of his own. He might assault your character, become defensive, stonewall, or he might get disgusted that you can't reasonably assert yourself without resorting to an attack.

If you want to avoid making this foul, talk about his behavior, not his self. Talk only about what you know, the things you are an expert on. Talk about just how annoying that toilet paper roll can be and why you cannot just switch it around your way when you use it.

Chapter 14
The Second Foul:
Defensiveness

When you're having a fight, you've got to put your dukes up, block his punches and attack when you can because the best defense is a good offense. But, when you're trying to have a constructive discussion, defensiveness, and a defensive offensive, is one of the worse things you can do. It's the second of the fouls to look out for.

Here's some examples:

"Honey," she says. "Did you call Betty and Ralph to let them know that we're not coming tonight?"

If you're going to be defensive, you might answer:

"Do you know how busy my day was? Why didn't you just do it?"

Rather than:

"No."

Here's another example.

If he says, "I'm worried about our spending. We only have so much money and every time you go to the store, you come home with twice as much as you went for. Do you really need a hundred-and-forty-three pairs of shoes?"

Being defensive, you say:

"My spending! Did you ever look at your spending? How much beer did you go through last week?"

Or…

"I bring in more than half of our income. I should be able to spend it as I want."

Rather than:

"I'm sorry, I didn't know money was so tight. You know, since I started working so much and you started paying the bills, I got out of touch with how we're doing, financially."

How 'bout this one?

When she says, "You're a selfish lout! You never think of anyone but yourself!"

You say, "Well, you're a nagging bitch and you have control issues!"

When you could say, "That's defamation. A foul. Can we start over? Can you give me specific examples?"

To spot defensiveness, listen for someone concerned with finding blame, rather than solutions. Look for one posing as a victim and seeking sympathy, rather than rolling up his sleeves and getting to work.

A lot of times when you're being defensive, you're concerned that if your partner wins the argument, you lose. You're attempting to testify to the truth, set things right, correct the record. You believe you're the injured party here. You're as mad as hell; you won't take it anymore. You'd rather be right, than have a good relationship. You'd rather open up a hundred other problems than look at the one on the table.

Defensiveness is frequently a secondary foul; a response to another foul. Often defamation precedes it. It's a response to a rapid devolving conversation. Your character is being attacked, so you defend it. It's only natural. Unfortunately, two wrongs do not make a right. If it did, we'd all be completely squared away by now.

The antidote to defensiveness is to take responsibility for something, anything, even if you don't think the problem is primarily yours.

"Did I call Betty and Ralph? No, I'm sorry. I said I would, but I got busy and it slipped my mind."

See, now you can call them, solve the problem at hand, and move on to other issues, like the fact that all day you're too busy to call your friends.

Chapter 15
The Third Foul:
Stonewalling

Stonewalling is when you or your partner communicate or cooperate about as well as a stone wall. It's pointless to have a conversation with a stone wall; and unnecessary to be one. It's the third foul to avoid if you want to have a constructive conversation.

Listen for these words: *Fine... Whatever... Sure... Later...I'll try...Sort of...Not now...Yes, Dear... I never said that...*, if you want to distinguish a stone wall from a responsive human being.

Listen for the passive voice behind which stonewalling partners, governments, and corporations hide from responsibility. "Mistakes were made..."

Pay attention for deflection, sparse responses, or outright refusal to answer questions.

Watch for lack of eye contact, a brief conversation, vagueness, non-commitment.

CONSTRUCTIVE CONFLICT

It's easy to mistake a person stonewalling for someone out of touch with his emotions or someone with low verbal skills. To tell the difference, you've got to see them in other circumstances. Can he express his feelings when his football team loses? Can she talk for hours with her girlfriends? If they can, but they are not doing it with you, they are stonewalling.

Stonewalling usually occurs when the stonewaller is flooded. Now, there's a mixed metaphor for you. I'm talking about being flooded by emotions, when you have so many emotions going on, you don't know how you feel because you're feeling so many things. Flooding also occurs when the emotions are so strong, you're afraid to do anything or say anything because it would probably be the wrong thing. Flooding emotions can overwhelm all good sense.

It's a pretty good idea to shut the hell up when you are flooded before you make everything worse. I recommend it to people. Having a period to cool down is a great way to forestall fights; and, provided you ever return to the issue, it's a better way to resolve differences. Why do I sometimes call it a foul, then? What is the difference between shutting the hell up because you are flooded and stonewalling?

The difference is in the notification.

If you get flooded when you talk with your partner take a break, by all means; but give some notification to tell him that's what you're doing. Memorize the following phrases: *Let's take a break... Time Out... Let's cool down... Let me think...This is going badly... I'll get back to you in a minute...* before you get silent, evasive, or walk away. This way your partner know what's going on. All you have to do is say one of those phrases and you are absolved from the guilt of stonewalling. Provided you don't abuse the privilege, that is.

If your partner asks for a break when he is flooded, please, please give it to him. Nothing good ever comes when you persist in an argument after flooding occurs, even if you think he is abusing his break-taking privileges. Abuse of break-taking should be an issue discussed at another time, not added on to the argument you are already having.

Some couples have trouble taking breaks when they need to. Once their adrenaline gets going, they don't back down for nothin'. They won't ask for a break and they won't grant one. Some china has to be smashed or blood spilled before they will stop.

In those cases, it's important to recognize flooding and take a break earlier. Some couples like that are better off having their difficult conversations in public places if that environment is likely to restrain them, or with a referee. If that doesn't work, they're better off with an order of protection.

How much time do you need for a break? Twenty minutes, tops, provided you didn't spend your break stewing or rehearsing zingers. That's not really a break, is it? An effective break can be very short. Check your pulse when you begin and end the break when it slows down.

Another thing I recommend for couples who have had problems with stonewalling is the establishment of a safe word. At the beginning of the conversation, agree on some word you don't use commonly. *Oklahoma* is a good one if you don't live in Oklahoma. Having an easy way out of a difficult conversation has a paradoxical effect on people. When you know you can easily stop a painful conversation, you are more likely to go forward with it. It eliminates the need for stonewalling.

So stonewalling is often used to help manage flooding. If you're stonewalling when you are not flooded, then you have a serious problem. You need to think about whether you are capable of love or if your relationship is more about retaining power and control. You need to think about whether you are a reasonable human with feelings, or an inanimate, inert, immovable object.

Chapter 16
The Fourth Foul:
Contempt

Of all the four fouls of an unfair fight, contempt is the most damaging. It's the *coup de grace* that finishes off a relationship. If you were wondering if you should see a marriage counselor, if contempt shows up: you should; but it may be too late.

You can recognize contempt in its various forms. There's the milder versions: eye rolling, sneering, sarcasm, an exasperated sigh. There's the stronger types: name calling, mockery, scorn, and the pulling out of all the dirty laundry. Contempt is implicit in domestic violence, back stabbing, betrayal, and when you alienate him from his children.

Contempt is found whenever you communicate that you're superior to your partner; each time you cut him down, objectify him, overpower him, ridicule him, and undermine his relationship with others. Express contempt when you're trying to have a constructive conversation, and it's lights out. There's no point in going on. It's time to take a break and you'll need to apologize when and if you return.

The four fouls, Defamation, Defensiveness, Stonewalling, and Contempt, can be thought of on a continuum, ranging from the most cerebral, Defamation, to the most visceral, Contempt. Contempt is associated with the disgust you feel when you are sick to your stomach, poisoned by some toxic substance, and you puke. When you are showing contempt you are basically saying that the love of your life is a toxic substance and you can't wait to get rid of her. That's a peculiar expression of love, isn't it?

We might differ on what we believe love is; for some there is more passion than others. Nevertheless, I think we can all agree that love has to involve admiration, appreciation, attraction, and respect. Contempt corrodes all that. Yet, I never fail to be amazed when couples can show contempt for one another and then insist that they are in love.

However, despite what we think love should be like, as a matter of fact, love and hate are close cousins in the family of emotions, unrelated to apathy and indifference. You can be the most hateful of the very people you love. It's impossible to be indifferent to your partner, it matters what she does. The people you are closest to are the very people you can most easily hurt, and who can most easily hurt you.

If you're going to love people, you're just going to have to get used to the fact that sometimes you'll have contempt for them, and they will for you. Your darling may disgust you, but it is a feeling that can be regulated.

All you have to do is get close to someone and you can see all his flaws. There are blemishes on his skin; his feet look like they belong in a monster movie. He sniffles and snorts and farts and burps and leaves skid marks on his laundry. He's afraid of spiders, cries at graduations, lies to his mother, and is too cowed by his boss to ask him for a raise. Sometimes his penis fails to get hard. He has complexes, phobias, insecurities, and, once in a while, has bad dreams from which he awakes, screaming. He's filled with rage when a car cuts him off. Your partner is a mess.

So are you.

Contempt shows up whenever you forget that you are just as disgusting as your partner. When you fail to observe the truce that is necessary for any two people to get together. When you misplaced an agreement to overlook obvious and not so obvious defects. Contempt shows up when you fail to keep your promise to love him anyway.

The thing that regulates contempt is humility. Nurture your humility. Those who fail to, get humiliated..

Chapter 17
Don't be Evil

If you are unfamiliar with the reality of evil in the world, watch the news. If you're unfamiliar with its presence in yourself, ask your wife.

Or husband. Partners know very well how evil we can be . We can be evil to the people we love in ways we never imagined being evil to anyone else.

There's even a term for it that we marriage counselors use: normal marital sadism. Sadism means that you get pleasure out of inflicting pain on another. Marital, in this case, means any close, committed relationship, including marriage. Normal means you do it. Add it up and it means you enjoy inflicted pain on your partner.

Who, me?

Yes, you. You don't have to commit violence to be a sadist. Have you ever gotten even, held a grudge, let go of (rather than lost) your temper, picked a fight, withheld sex, or felt justified and entitled to retribution when your feelings were hurt?

Of course you have.

What is that, if it's not evil? It's deliberately done when you could have chosen not to. It's primitive, punitive, petty and vindictive. You know where his buttons are, so you push them. You know where his skeletons are buried, so you dig them up. You perversely derive satisfaction from making him squirm. Screwing with people's minds is fun. Face it, it's evil.

Even God-fearing, peace-loving, romantic types who never seem to fight, engage in covert combat. Especially them. The brighter the light, the darker the shadow.

To be sure, there are some who are more evil in their relationships than others. If you want to learn to spot them before you get hitched to them, look for someone who does not act like an adult. Marriage is for adults only. Not everyone over the age of eighteen is an adult. Many, very many, are immature. They will not take responsibility, cannot comfort themselves, seek instant gratification, and need other people to be better before they can be. You can't take them anywhere because if they are not in the right environment, if you don't affirm them enough, everything goes to hell. People who don't handle frustrations well, who take things personally, will cause mayhem all over the place in the name of self-preservation.

You might expect that this evil would happen if the relationship was weak or if you didn't care about your partner. Actually, weakness or lack of importance has nothing to do with it. You can expect this behavior when your alliance alarm goes off.

Remember the alliance alarm? That feeling you get when you perceive your partner is not there for you? There's a lot of things you might do when your alliance alarm goes off, but one of the most popular is to punish your partner for whatever transgression you think she committed. So, you are sadistic to your loved one because you want you to be closer.

That's whacked.

So, chill out, let it go, tell her how you feel, and don't hurt her back, even if she deserves it. Don't be evil.

CONSTRUCTIVE CONFLICT

Chapter 18
Repair the Damage

If you've been reading the last few chapters, you now know how to have a constructive conflict. You can pick the right time and place to talk about difficult matters. You start with the easy stuff. You pay no attention to the alarm going off in your head. You don't expect her to fix the things she has no influence over. You know what you're asking. You can learn from her and how to acknowledge her feelings. You can call the four fouls of an unfair fight, whether you commit them or she does; and you know enough not to be evil. You've learned a lot, but, before you and your partner can perfect your new skills, things can still go badly.

You need to learn when and how to make repairs.

Remember the last time you and your partner tried to have a conversation, but it turned into a fight? Go through the scenes carefully. Get to the part right when it started to get ugly. Now rewind back a few frames to where no one was mad yet. Roll it in slow motion. Watch the expression change in your partner's face as you say that thing you said that made her so upset. You see it? You see that look? You know the look. You've seen it plenty of times, whenever you've been in trouble. Memorize it. When you see that look again, stop whatever you're doing and make a repair.

If you were driving down the highway and your tire blew, you wouldn't go on cruising, playing the radio, looking at the sights, as if nothing was wrong. No, you'd stop and fix it. The same principle applies when you begin to have a fight with your partner. Stop talking about whatever it is you were talking about and reaffirm your commitment to the relationship.

So, let's say you're trying to convince him to get up with the baby once in a while. Your cause is just. You have to go to work in the morning just like he does. You need your sleep as much as him. Spending time with the baby, even at two o'clock in the morning, can be a tremendously rewarding experience that facilitates bonding. Furthermore, the evidence of his failure to pull his weight is unassailable. You've been keeping track. You even have a chart. You wait for a good time to talk, you clear your throat, and speak. You make your point, but then, there's that look on his face that I told you to notice. It's time to make a repair.

You might know what you did to get that look. Maybe you just couldn't resist a little jab. Maybe his precious male ego got jostled too much. Maybe he took something the wrong way. Maybe he's overwhelmed. It doesn't matter why you got the look, you still need to make a repair.

It also doesn't matter how correct your complaint might be. A righteous cause does not guarantee that you've expressed it well, nor does it justify any means to implement it. You don't have to back away from the point you made; he still should get up with the baby. Don't forget the whole thing because he gave you the look, but you're going to have to live with this man, even if you win the debate and prevail over him. You're going to need his cooperation, even if he agrees with you. Make the repair.

If you see that look, stop trying to make your point. You made it already. The job is done. Continue in the same vein and it'll just get ugly. You need to make a repair.

Did I say that already?

It's not necessary at this juncture to fix everything about your relationship. You're just trying to undo whatever just happened and get the conversation back on a track. Correct the little things before they turn into big things. Switch your focus from content to process. Forget about what you are trying to say and pay attention to how you are saying it. If you see that look, you're saying it wrong. Stop it. Make the... you guessed it... make the repair.

People often ask me, "OK, I saw that look and I stopped. Now what do I do to repair the damage?"

You're asking me how to love your husband? That's something you should already know, he became your husband somehow. Go back to that tape you were looking at. Rewind it to the beginning of your relationship. Look at how charming you were then, how easy you were to get along with, how you guys talked for hours. Look at all the ways you won him over and made him decide you were the one for him. Do that again. That's how you make a repair.

Now is the time to paraphrase, use your safe word, take a break, focus on the positive, reset and reboot.

There's also humor, humility, a gentle touch, a come-hither look, a soft expression. Sometimes you don't have to say anything to make a repair, but you do need to communicate that you love him.

In my experience, couples know very well how to make repairs; they just don't do it. Or they don't notice when their partner is attempting to make one. They get stuck on the issue, rather than paying attention to how they are talking about it.

CONSTRUCTIVE CONFLICT

Don't wait until doors are slammed before you stop trying to hammer home the point. Notice your relationship needs mending. Make a repair.

CONSTRUCTIVE CONFLICT

Chapter 19
Let Your Partner Repair the Damage

Remember the last time you and your partner tried to have a conversation, but it turned into a fight? Go through the scenes carefully. Get to the part right when it started to get ugly. Now go forward a few frames, **after** where you got mad. Roll it in slow motion. Maybe your partner tried to make a repair. Making a repair is a crucial step whether you're doing it or your partner.

See how charming he was just then, how easy he might have been to get along with if you had noticed the repair attempt. He might've paraphrased, used your safe word, took a break, focused on the positive, reset and rebooted. There could've been humor, humility, a gentle touch, a come-hither look, a soft expression. You were mad, so you might not have noticed it, but he was trying to communicate that he loves you.

If you were driving down the highway, your tire blew, and your partner stopped to fix it, you wouldn't put the car in gear and go driving off while he was trying to fix it. No, you could kill someone that way. You may be angry and having a fight, but you're not homicidal. The same principle applies when your partner tries to end a fight. Stop talking about whatever it is you were talking about and join him in reaffirming your commitment to the relationship.

It also doesn't matter how correct your point of view might be. A righteous cause does not guarantee that you've expressed it well, nor does it justify any means to implement it. You don't have to back away from the point you made. Don't forget the whole thing because he tried to make a repair, because you're going to have to live with this man, even if you win the debate and prevail over him. You're going to need his cooperation, even if he agrees with you. Join him in making the repair.

It's not necessary at this juncture to fix everything about your relationship. The two of you are just trying to undo whatever just happened and get the conversation back on a track. Join him in correcting the little things before they turn into big things. Switch your focus from content to process. Forget about what you are trying to say and pay attention to how you are saying it. If you see that look, you're saying it wrong. Stop it. Make the... you guessed it... make the repair.

No one has ever asked me, "How do I let my partner repair the damage?"

You don't have to do anything. All you have to do is notice he's trying to make it right and stop your part of the fight.

Don't wait until doors are slammed before you stop trying to hammer home the point. Notice your relationship needs mending. If he's started to make a repair, let him.

CONSTRUCTIVE CONFLICT

Chapter 20
Detect Dreams

You find yourself gridlocked. You want children; she doesn't. He wants you to go to church, but you're an atheist. She likes to stay home; you're always ready to party. There doesn't seem to be any solution. There's no way to compromise. You're ready to call it quits. What do you do?

Step away from the problem.

Look at the big picture. Understand the different points of view. Not just your perspectives on the immediate issue, but what lies behind them. Behind every position is a dream or a value that you and your partner find essential. Acknowledging and respecting these deepest, most personal hopes and dreams is the key to getting past the impasse.

To get out of gridlock, you have to understand what causes people to become rigid and inflexible. No matter what the issue, whether it's momentous, like following a job to a different state, or trivial, like how to make the bed, deadlock is an indication that there are dreams and values that have not been identified, acknowledged, or respected.

You didn't survive childhood without coming away with some ideas of what you would like to do differently than your parents and what you would like to do the same. These ideas could cover marriage, childrearing, vocation, or general matters of lifestyle. If your father was violent, you may have had your fill of it in childhood and be determined not repeat the behavior in your life. If your family always had Sunday dinner and you found this was the anchor that kept everyone from going adrift, you may have an unwavering commitment to Sunday dinners.

You didn't enter adulthood without being aware, more or less, that the time you have is limited. You want to make your life worthwhile. You want to make a difference. You came up with ideas of things you could do: help people, raise children, glorify God, experience life, pursue truth, or create beauty; things you can do to contribute.

These resolutions, the ones you bring from childhood and the ones you make in the face of death, are very powerful. They define who you are and what makes your life worthwhile. Your partner has them, too. Do you know what they are?

CONSTRUCTIVE CONFLICT

When I say be a dream detective, I mean that you need to know what your partner's dreams and resolutions are and how they impact the issue at hand. It may be that the way she makes the bed matters more and for a deeper reason than you ever imagined. It may be that being a good Catholic, or a staunch atheist, is vital to his identity.

Consider the conflict that you have, take her position and trace back to where it connects to these resolutions. When you go back that far, you often find that there are many ways of accomplishing the dream. It turns out that she makes the bed that way because it's how her Grandmother made her bed. She loved her Grandmother, whose home was an orderly haven from the chaos she grew up in. She is determined to not let her home be chaotic. Well, there are lots of ways to hold off chaos. The way she makes the bed may not be as crucial once others ways are found.

When you are able to trace the conflict back to the value that mades the conflict important, then you can come up with other solutions that accomplish the same goal. When you know these things about your loved one, you can't help but respect them. It's what makes her, her. You want her to succeed and accomplish her dreams because, well, what is love if it's not that?

CONSTRUCTIVE CONFLICT

Chapter 21
Compromise

Compromise is one of those things, like flossing, that everyone says is desirable and few are willing to do. We mostly want our partner to practice it. However, you don't really need to be so cagy about compromise. Just say you don't like it and avoid it when you can.

There are good and bad ways to evade compromising. Here are all the ways I can think of, in no particular order. You'll have to decide for yourself which ones are good and which are bad. I will say that all these methods can be effective; in the short term, at least.

First, there's screaming and shouting, hitting and gouging, whining and cajoling, sarcasm and name calling. What you're going to want to do is to take whatever your loved one wants and increase the cost for him, so that he will give up on it. Domestic violence is the most crude form of this method. The most successful users of intimidation never raise a hand in anger, they are able to terrorize and threaten their partners into compliance by more subtle means.

The second method to avoid compromise is equally popular. You can give the appearance of agreement to whatever she wants, with no intention of ever following through. This stops the discussion long enough so that you can watch the game. Repeat for as long as it takes her to give up on it.

If your partner doesn't like to compromise (who does?), you may be able to collude with him into pretending the problem doesn't exist.

One counterintuitive method of avoiding compromise is to just let her have her way. This spares you the hard work of being real about what you need and coming to terms with the fact that you and your partner just may not be compatible. Sure, you lose whatever you give up, but you can always make up for it later by nursing grudges and exacting concessions. A good grudge is better than drugs.

Blackmail.

You might be able to evade compromise if you have a plural marriage. You can form a coalition with your sister wives and vote your husband into submission.

If you don't have a plural marriage, you can create sort of a temporary one by erasing the boundaries between your union and others. Friends, children, in-laws, and marriage counselors can be enlisted to arbitrate disputes. The wise ones will refuse, but you don't need wisdom from them; you just need them to go along with you. You can get your whole family to gang up on your wife and call it an intervention.

You can avoid a lot of compromise by having a traditional, paternalistic marriage. Just put the husband in charge of all the decision making. Line up all the machinery of society: social disapproval, family ties, religious strictures, the power of the state, to support him and ensure his way or the highway. Both men and women may like this arrangement for their own reasons. The men, so they can be in charge, and the women, so the men can. I suppose it can work just as well the other way around, with the wife in charge, if you can get society to go along with it. The ship has not yet completely sailed when it comes to paternalism in our society. Some say that a new ship, maternalism, has been spotted coming into port.

Let's not forget that, before you compromise, you can play a game of marital chicken. Stick to your point to see if the other side blinks first.

So, let's see. Are there other ways to avoid compromising?

If you've been trying my suggestions about having a constructive conflict, you might've found that you and your partner don't disagree as much as you used to. There are huge regions of concord you never knew existed. You might have discovered your partner just wants to be taken seriously. He needs to be heard, that's all. So, see, no compromise needed.

Make a deal; do some horse trading.

If one partner has special expertise in a particular area of common life, you could give that person the final word in matters pertaining. She's good with figures, so she makes the final decision on money issues. Since he's a teacher and is an expert on child development, he makes the call with the kids.

Split the difference.

Even when there's no expertise, per se, as a practical matter, it can make sense when each partner deals with his or her own stuff. You could be vested in the ultimate authority when it comes to your own job, your own kids, your family of origin, your car, so on and so forth. In the same way, couples who do not put their money in a common pot, but handle it individually often have one partner retain control over their portion of the income.

It's possible to break up the functions of marital life in as many pieces as you would like and maintain dozens of small, petty dictatorships over the laundry, the vacuuming, making breakfast, writing checks, etc. You could cede to the other partner a significant advisory role, but the final decision is left to the person in charge. Many traditional marriages are structured in this way. Husbands have the final say making a living and relating to the outside world, while wives rule inside the home. This arrangement has its advantages in clarifying roles, but heaven help you if you lose your partner and you don't know where he did his banking, or if your wife picked out all your clothes and now you don't know how to shop.

Here's another way to settle an impasse and avoid compromise. Go with whomever has the strongest feelings on the subject. If he's a long-suffering Chicago Cubs fan and they're finally in the World Series, there's no question of what you're tuning in to if you don't care what you watch. If she can't digest Indian food or wash the curry smell out of her hair, you may have to go without your fix of vindaloo. This method works well when you and your partner are in good faith, are not unnecessarily histrionic, and don't really mind your emotions, much less someone else's, making all major decisions. Otherwise, the biggest baby will always win.

Take turns giving in.

If you don't like any of these choices, remember, compromise is not necessary if you don't care about the relationship, or if you care about it, but not as much as you care about the Stanley Cup Finals, or shopping for shoes, or sending your children to Catholic school, or seeing your parents on Christmas morning, or having the right to drink beer until you're passed out on the couch after having barfed all over yourself and yelled at the kids. There are plenty of things that you might believe are more important than keeping your vows to the love of your life. If you really believe that, then do not compromise your beliefs by compromising. Stick to your guns, wave the flag, and never give up.

So, you see, there're lots of choices before you have to compromise. If you don't like any of them, then hold your nose, grit your teeth, and just do it.

Chapter 22
Commemorate

If you and your partner succeed in having a difficult conversation and come away with something resolved, there's one more thing you need to do before you are done.

Remember it.

You don't want to have to cover that ground again.

There are some couples who have the same fight over and over. Each time, they settle it somehow, but the next time they don't remember what they decided. Or they remember things differently. Then they argue over who remembered what.

It's far better, when you are basking in the warm glow of a successful negotiation, to immediately write down what you decided. Think of it as the minutes from a board meeting, or an amendment to a marital constitution, or as an important contract. The key is to commit it to writing and put it in a safe place where you can refer to it later.

You may want to keep a file just for this purpose. In the file you keep all your agreements so you can find them if you need them.

Many people resist writing things down because they want their relationship to be a dynamic living thing, not a dry, legalistic business arrangement. Well, writing things down doesn't have to mean that you can't revise it if you need to, if you follow due process. Your relationship can still breathe. Think of these documents as the bones of a body that give it structure, definition, and strength. Think of them as the bass line of music, upon which the band builds harmonies. They're like the laws of physics, which underwrite all beauty, motion, and grace; or, the Periodic Table of the Elements, which which enables us to understand chemistry.

Also, there's something about committing things to writing that forces people to be more precise. The devil's in the details, so you may want to work them out now, while you and your partner are on a roll, rather than when they emerge later.

Commemoration also involves doing something fun. Celebrating your accomplishment. I suppose that's what make-up sex is all about, but it doesn't have to stop there. Have make-up sex, by all means, but also consider going out to dinner, taking a vacation, renewing your vows. Go to the hardware store, buy a hatchet, and take it out in the backyard and bury it. Create or designate some kind of a symbol of your new agreement: a work of art or a piece of furniture, some jewelry, plant a tree. Have something that you can point to and say, this is a sign of your new covenant, an emblem of the renewal of love.

You and your partner just accomplished something important. You took a conflict that could have driven you apart, you wrestled with it while maintaining respect for each other. This is the kind of operation that, if done enough, can save the world. Give yourself some credit, pat yourself on the back, and celebrate. Make this success something that you will never forget.

CONSTRUCTIVE CONFLICT

Chapter 23
Practice

How can reading a book help you have constructive conflicts? It can't.

You can't learn to play tennis by reading, either. You've got to play.

I took tennis lessons once. The coach asked me to show him my serve. I hit a few. I looked over and saw him shake his head.

"We have a lot of work to do," he said.

First, he had me put my racquet down and practice tossing the ball. He showed me what I was doing wrong. I was bending my elbow, causing the ball the ball to go behind me where I couldn't hit it well. He showed me how to toss it right.

"Keep that elbow straight," he said.

He watched me toss the ball until I did it correctly.

"There," he said. "Now toss it that way two thousand times, then it'll be automatic."

CONSTRUCTIVE CONFLICT

My tennis coach understood how to effect change. First, he had to break down the process of serving a tennis ball into parts small enough for me to focus. Just the toss. Then, he knew that to break old bad habits and create new ones it is necessary to repeat the new habit over and over again. How many times? I don't know if two thousand times is the precise number necessary. Suffice it to say, it's a lot.

So, if you take this process and apply it, not to serving a tennis ball, but to the way to manage conflict, you can see there's a lot of work to do. First, you must know how to manage conflict and compare it to what you've been doing. You have to know how to do it right to know what you're doing wrong. Then you have to practice doing it right, over and over again, until it's automatic.

Let's say you're prone to stonewalling. You've read Chapter Thirteen and understood why you, all of a sudden, shut down. You've agreed on a safe word with your partner and know enough to use it when you get flooded, emotionally. You know you're not supposed to just go off somewhere, without saying a word, or go off somewhere to stew. So, the next time you're having a discussion with the love of your life, you try some of these things and, guess what, it works! It was a very simple operation, as simple as tossing a tennis ball while keeping your arm straight. If you did it once, you've achieved a small victory. If you do it two-thousand times, you've changed a bad habit into a good one. It may now be automatic.

It would take me about less than half an hour to toss a tennis ball correctly two-thousand times, thus creating a good habit quite easily. It's not so easy when you train yourself to use your safe word. You would have to have two-thousand difficult conversations and two-thousand incidents of emotional flooding. That could take years. This is one reason why so many people relapse, so many people say change is impossible, and so many people give up. But, change is possible. It just takes persistence.

By the way, my tennis coach went on to show me other things I could use to improve my game, but what really stuck with me was how to perfect the toss. That was the only thing I learned from those tennis lessons. It turns out, that's all I needed to learn so that I could beat the people I was likely to play. If I ever turn pro, I'll have to see the tennis coach again to learn the right way to actually hit the ball. The same thing goes with learning constructive conflict. Very small changes, if they're the right changes, can make a huge difference. But you've got to play.

CONSTRUCTIVE CONFLICT

Chapter 24
If You Need More Help

Reading this book may not be enough to get you and your partner on the right track to constructively use your conflicts. If you need more help and live near the Rochester, New York area, I may be able to meet with you. If you don't, then begin the search for a good therapist. I wish I could say that choosing a good therapist is a simple matter, but it's not. Licenses and certifications can only tell you which kind of school or trainings the therapist went to, they cannot tell you anything about their competence beyond the minimal level. You're left to the recommendations of others, or to follow your own instincts.

If you prefer reading to seeing a therapist, there are books I can suggest; although, if you do a lot of reading on the subject, you'll see why I wanted to give you my own take. Much of the material in this book comes from family therapy theoreticians who have preceded me. They seldom get along. If you want to see for yourself, look at the books and websites from the bibliography following this chapter; but, let me give you a little guidance on what you'll find.

My chief source is David Schnarch, and what he calls Crucible® Therapy. Let's get one thing out of the way about Schnarch. Yes, he has a funny name. Although, I must admit that, as a person with a very ordinary name, Wilson, I feel a little jealous of him. It's distinctive, at least.

Schnarch didn't come up with these ideas solely on his own, either; although he did give them his own clever turns of phrase, and trademark them so no one else can use them. He built on a foundation first laid by Murray Bowen, one of the pioneers of family therapy. While Bowen is not a household name, even in households comprised of shrinks, he gave us such widely used concepts as boundaries, triangles, ideas about the influence of sibling position, and the differentiation of the self. All right, maybe differentiation of the self is not a widely used concept, but it's a key concept, having to do with growing up and acting like an adult.

Bowen is the closest thing I have to a guru, although I've never been one to hand myself over completely to a guru and make his or her ideas and methods my own without adding my own idiosyncratic twists. I only keep the parts that work for me and that seem to resonate with the people who come to me for counseling.

For me, Bowen provides much of the theoretical framework for how I work with conflict. The Gottmans help with the application. The Gottmans, a husband and wife team from Seattle, are known for their painstaking empirical research of marital behavior. Where others who write about relationships pull their ideas out of thin air, or from some part of their anatomy, the Gottmans conducted interviews with ninety-five newlyweds and followed them for years. They not only listened to what those couples had to say, they also scrutinized physical data taken during those interviews: heart rate, sweating, skin temperature, and microexpressions. They paid attention to how these couples fought and noted how they made up, if they did. The Gottmans collected the best data we have on the predictors of divorce.

As you might expect from those who take a geeky approach to determining truth, little of Gottmania has made its way into the popular culture. They're not the people to go to if you are looking for sweeping theoretical constructs or whopping generalizations. They're the people you want to quote if you want to be right.

The second set of sources, Johnson, Bowlby, and Ainsworth, also come from the family therapy field, but they're largely antithetical from the first, Schnarch, Bowen, and Gottman, so that you seldom hear anyone mentioning them all together. Sue Johnson has her *Emotionally Focused Couple Therapy*, which she constructed out of research done by John Bowlby and his assistant, Mary Ainsworth. Bowlby and Ainsworth did psychology a huge favor in the middle of the last century by informing us that people need people. This was seen as radical and was thoroughly rejected until orphan babies began dying in Romania due to the lack of human contact. Those orphan babies, together with Bowlby and Ainsworth, gave us attachment therapy and launched a thousand quizzes in which people identified whether they were securely attached, anxious-avoidant insecurely attached, anxious-resistant insecurely attached, or just disorganized and confused as all get out.

The problem with using all this attachment theorizing has been that it involves applying child psychology to adults. In contrast, the Bowen school believes that, if you're an adult, you should act like one and set aside childish things like the need to be mothered, nurtured, and affirmed. A lot of problems happen in your relationships when you will not take responsibility, cannot comfort yourself, seek instant gratification, and need other people to be better before you can be. To that, I say Amen.

If the Bowenites can be said to just want people to grow up, the Bowlby-ites counter with, as much as you think you can grow up, deep inside you'll always be a dependent child. You could be the highest functioning person in the world, but when it's late at night and you're

117

tired, you'll turn into a cranky two-year-old. The same will happen when you're sick, or your dog dies, or when you get so adult that you're living in an adult care facility. It'll certainly happen if your spouse threatens to leave, or if you feel betrayed by her. The Bowlby-ites say, in essence, let's get real, no one ever enters a relationship ready for one, there's always a lot of work to do. It can only be done in an atmosphere of love, tolerance, and patience. Amen to that, too.

Anyone who is caught up in the controversy between the Bowenites and Bowlby-ites will think I'm saying Amen out of both sides of my mouth, but I'm only affirming the truth wherever I see it. If you read much in family therapy, you'll find there is a lot of conflict there, too, as well as in families. You might wonder, *Can't they get along?* You might say, *They should be able to get along because they purport to teach getting along to others.*

If you do think that, then I have failed you in writing this book. The main point I've been trying to make is that relationships put you in conflict. That's their purpose. You're supposed to be in conflict with your loved ones, and people who write about family therapy are supposed to be in conflict with one another. If it's well regulated conflict, then conflict is how we all get better. The family therapy field is a rock tumbler, too; just like your love relationship. Conflict knocks the rough edges off of all our theories.

That's what I call constructive conflict.

More Resources

Ainsworth

Krumwiede, Andreas; *Attachment Theory According to John Bowlby and Mary Ainsworth;* GRIN Verlag; 2014

Bowen

Bowen, Murray and Kerr, Michael E; *Family Evaluation;* W. W. Norton; 1988

Bowen, Murray; *Family Therapy in Clinical Practice;* Jason Aronson, Incorporated; 1978

www.thebowencenter.org

Bowlby

Bowlby, John; *Attachment and Loss;* Basic Books; 1982

Bowlby, John; *A Secure Base: Clinical Applications of Attachment Theory, Psychology Press; 1988*

Gottman

Gottman, John & Silver, Nan; *The Seven Principles for Making Marriage Work: A Practical Guide from the Country's Foremost Relationship Expert;* Potter/TenSpeed/Harmony, 1999

Gottman, John; *The Relationship Cure;* Random House, 2002

www.gottman.com

Johnson

Johnson, Sue; *Hold Me Tight;* Little, Brown and Company; 2009

Johnson, Sue; *Love Sense*, Little; Brown and Company; 2013

www.drsuejohnson.com

Snarch

Snarch, David; *Intimacy & Desire: Awaken the Passion in Your Relationship;* Beaufort Books; 2011

Snarch, David; *Passionate Marriage: Keeping Love and Intimacy Alive in Committed Relationships;* W. W. Norton & Company; 2009

www.crucibletherapy.com

Wilson

The website of my private practice-

www.keithwilsoncounseling.com

My blog about mental health and relationship issues, Madness 101 - www.keithwilsoncounseling.wordpress.com

Two books of fiction

Wilson, Keith; *Intersections*; The Narrative Imperative Press, 2015

Wilson, Keith; *Fate's Janitors: Moping Up Madness at a Mental Health Clinic*; Createspace, 2010

www.aboutme.keithwilsonpage.com

If you want to get in touch with me, email me at keithwilsoncounseling@gmail.com.

Made in the USA
Middletown, DE
21 October 2015